RED SHIFT

P. Inman

ROOF

Parts of "Red Shift" appeared in *"Language" Poetries*, edited by Douglas Messerli and published by New Directions; "Waver" was published as *Abacus* #18, edited by Peter Ganick. The author wishes to thank the editors.

This book was made possible, in part, by grants from the National Endowment for the Arts and the New York State Council on the Arts.

Production by Diane Ward and Susan Bee
Cover design by Diane Ward
Author photo by Quinn Robinson

ISBN 0-937804-28-2
Library of Congress Catalog Card Number 87-063135

ROOF BOOKS
are published by
The Segue Foundation
300 Bowery
New York, N.Y. 10012

Contents

"decker"

for tina

(pg. 1)

mute,　think,　　　off,　　bleed

＿＿＿＿＿＿＿＿＿＿＿＿＿

daughter
chicory

hem off
keag

＿＿＿＿＿＿＿＿＿＿＿＿＿
＝＝＝＝＝＝＝＝＝＝＝＝＝

(pg. 2)

eyeds,
dreg,
daint

＿＿＿＿＿＿＿＿＿＿＿＿＿
＝＝＝＝＝＝＝＝＝＝＝＝＝

(pg. 3)

diff–
　　　––earth

＿＿＿＿＿＿＿＿＿＿

mem,oir,　　　mengs
calumet
thicks no
day still
oyster abbe

quogue
leit　legs

7

‾‾‾‾‾‾‾‾‾‾‾‾‾‾
‾‾‾‾‾‾‾‾‾‾‾‾‾‾

moeb egg

‾‾‾‾‾‾‾‾‾‾‾‾‾‾

seabed off at thigh.
chalk prine.   noun cement.
    plinh(er).
  woman spoieriee.

‾‾‾‾‾‾‾‾‾‾‾‾‾‾
‾‾‾‾‾‾‾‾‾‾‾‾‾‾

(pg. 5)

speak in from black knock

g l a y s husk.

‾‾‾‾‾‾‾‾‾‾‾‾

man immense off clough.

‾‾‾‾‾‾‾‾‾‾‾‾

brokes caesura

. . .

weakener nog
on clarity

. . .

onlook its spay

‾‾‾‾‾‾‾‾‾‾‾‾‾‾
‾‾‾‾‾‾‾‾‾‾‾‾‾‾

(pg. 6)

sentence giddity.

————————

an odd down
  edges so.

mang red hair

————————
————————

(pg. 7)

(mound
    nor trogg
  cetera.)

nihil in lean.

(page) "there's the end

    of another word
(relaxant)
besides muttonchops."

————————
————————

(pg. 8)

painters
think on parch

————————

scener eulogy.

      pane matter.

meig crag.

        ——————————
        ——————————

                          (pg. 9)

    pour blown to sentences

        ——————————
        ——————————

                         (pg. 10)

whitecap eaction.   brokener mudd

      each off of traw

  glaces   errata.
   deepener   traction.
mount by hazeltine.

    ——————————

            badgers.
            black. apart.

               ntires, minuses.

            dictum oquois.

            ——————————

pent to

into prose

      spide,   dilm.
              (nonce
            cllasp.)

                  roar

                 drote

           clungs cription.

         thigh loom teacher
       too pale emedy

        ——————————
        ——————————

                                            (pg. 11)

       kintoi's
          emastic.

blowns open of medley, no seem to it.
    grog downer   a line
opening into doctrine,   "bent blood".

      slog tape   / /   pline in
                       tintern———

          eggwhite
            though peopled

        ——————————

                    pore/   bent/
                        than
                            once

            ———————————

                        tarr moyer;;

        chaw typee

            ============
            ============

                                        (pg. 12)

        cete. dredge.
    clae. moeys.

        clungs. ply. digm.
        spatter. tharw.

auk. dry. drews.

    ———————————

            nil its book ocean

    ———————————

        spliint,
    (slungs) lean in dicter
    (every of doubt)   ments elongation).

            ============
            ============

                                        (pg. 13)

        jack's blackberry allowance

                print dockery.
                drew , mang.

figment keeps to hum

off flection
. climb in
draw nints

        painting (thin tinuous).
)   potato's gray out of pore

———————————
———————————

(pg. 14)

loom too lents (the picture
of Williams lacks an anachronism,
blown open during the woods.

———————————
      . . .
don'ts flatness   mosque llwyd

———————————
———————————

(pg. 15)

skew out of name

      darnt llud.
        kier
        (pernot
           loyow.

     prose off stell

—————————

craw   dots.

"red shift"

for joan retallack

silos all by a stillness /   nells from bend, a boil allow /

clock odd rounded by person /   the pour in a wave off of sugar /

"roundheads overpass" /   surd balls. /   all that muscle in

blackboard, ocean propos /   did i read it on a page or look

ahead about print exactly alike /   divides (every) to a blue now or less of a forest /   all the time in a pause, pointed

inland /   lewt marsh add /   a date based on still air /

name can't stick all that treeline /   lemp synod /   how after

is all /   ever since "white blood", a rise etched at her /

how far back would an idea go /   palatine of paper

all the history she needed to put dollars by /   thune prell

/   any word won't read again. North's toss pea off /   added

musicians, large to the shoreline they face /   spid   line

charp. the name of an oldie balled up in its spelling /   ad-

verse action caucus /   a near New Hampshire as a single line pickerel think /   sunken sky to frizz /   up collapse /

divides to a blue leaned ink /   style is just each, the side

beneath dates /   coda geller /   the city-line of a personage

/   chest wall less as skelter /   "mour" "baleen" "in-

digo" /   indigo none each Cowper's gland /   mute wooler

cloud redded hair /   is just each hour about life after pro-

perty /   cleaned content /   spald tar.   eye peas /   treetops

only start the weather, moviegoer's height all dried out /

sense about aspirin /   tanned ice /   black earth (motch)

ability /   about a crimp each below would add a speak

dune over by a voice /   thill mang pea /   (slodd drapery)

bacon old with outside /   poon inuit /   happenstance salsa /

"brown fries". her fill of bled book /   mountains have a matter

/   she'll like someone at the beginning of a career when all

the edges rub off on her hands /   "teach stools" /   daze vel skull a wool off (sharpener whoiks.) /   fruitbowl covered

with grammar /   "what sound is" dissolved along a curve /

d o o r l i k e n ' t /   bent on a sea of turpentine. tongue

extacks. /   parred elapse /   "pursuant to 5 USC 7114" (sto-

mach under a film of hills) /   fists balled, not "bellamy"

milk cans collapse in ash ska /   the distant the sky is open,

"equal skin" /   a round gashed money /   thighs each grade be-

hind Monet, too named as the loved one's look /   the word that

Joan dried /   lipe wall /   liffey o'clock /   nil its book ocean

/   plain skulled volume blue alikes. oilrag dead to vowel

sauch eyeline /   didn't birth leave a mood /   sided swim,

lines outside /   fog dried to a speed /   picturing what

happens to my elbow /   olfact name. quirr all to foam /   why

do they look dimensional /   curlicue service /   creek limch

/   the number of times in going quiet /   clake distance

what does steach blood /   a white over leverage let into me /

lashes rounded none-to-people /   skin of one weather follow-

ing out a shadow /   where did i lose trace /   pie Follette /

Aleuts invent deuce court /   speech slurred on the outside /

ball of shoulder poured through /   corp boil /   spall semei lasted river adjective /   a man walks into whitened totals /

a mile behind a palm with round skin /   drawns pell. lauts

isle /   mud in Buffalo's other story /   liner spog, timed as a

gland /   "pale porkpie" isn't color /   Rameau used applause as

a kind of black spoon /   potato strick /   people about 1832 prose as one long stage direction /   how exact a volume open

to a place /   humped piano, shorelines equal by their over,

hayed down alors /   earth Gogh than truth /   stacked talk

to a soda (dipster) /   standing legged the wrong amount to

pronounce. page shows of its better midst /   sawtooth, dreth monied thigh wrapping a highway /   any red closed by a chap-

ter /   insect bite hospital /   bends look as apart for a minute

drawn on the Mohawk /   opera near an average. statement a

space between trees /   (dringe balk) /   the ocean glinted dully,

the color of an exaggeration /   the odds however they happen

map with doorhooks /   murdo eyelid /   an edge filled with

paving, painting out of milked weather /   "mauge" /   *cos* site /

able coulée in a row /   deal hood lengs. polk road data /

overs solid than ever /   stovepipe, chogue. the difference

in a name, hair brushed back /   trung murgy a browner asleep that's "weak beat" scenery /   curd plinch /   other skin al-

most placed /   clock gelb /   clang punted at all, gray once

how everything /   hold my breath of built bread /   lips under

the number of a style /   slows from appear. the next dim as

is now that the air sounds thinking about paged color

ceye lent volume /   mur stripe. /   still beside one line

ended chest by comparison /   lander anythings /   bone drake

anklet /   down the minimum from listens pigment hard of

exist /   hairline feck. catch by plussed ocean /   looking

at an all drunk up Rembrandt, hearing all at a time

skin okasp /   brother slowed down to one line at a time /

any red will be done off the other, pointing her piano

toward a pitcher of print /   milp. /   sideburn of a matter

stirred /   dirks ink forest oleate /   the flam on sanity /

yolk imogen. nowhere out to what is said /   maque nasp

broken nose under coffee /   scenery marked along by a pea /

they become others' handwriting sudded anywhere /   thigh

drail. lessness critch /   who knows about the air around

"Wheely Down"? /   mooted ocean Arkansas /   finished lake,

no length as to the white boiled inside /   "hall dropsy"

the outfielder broke stride the more i spoke /   bottle allowing

a red minus. deadener put to people /   leam mound, drur aniline

/   rrung lipstick /   blooded shire total ago /   boswell's

shut ink, number bodied mesa /   hairline upholstery /   brogue

flim (period any mere) /   based minuet diminished to a city tint quie'b /   he set it down until the time around him

changed /   the mozart they had heard shown the forest /   sparsen

drim (every as keeps) /   a hole had been cut into the canvas

for the $ /   glance whichever potato /   what did Gramsci

really think about Lenin /   noun nothing but counterpoint

badlands there at a time /   metaphor red to its minimum. the

last word of a pea /   salsa reductio /   grounder out of bent

color /   a large oil from listens. washed lake job /   bend in

loom headedness so much invents to moat /   dribe boiled /

mist exact to anything. worked by side no down alike

size of bargaining unit /   a sentence made of black river /

an egg described between, argument curved to log /   saltire

glay /   a line or said but for the adirondacks /   "teeth zips"

all how iced /   "paradise under women" full of people left

out too far /   knocked bloodstream /   hearn't maw smotes

giving every out a turn / keal clothier / Asian word found

in Canada. fog as still approach / carbonate per sum ginzo

/ "that's not writing it's bell curves" / endless appoints

/ tell are cliption (Tina's plausible hair. leather much

bank under the view) / eye crusts mowage druff occupé

sump Deppe /   their onlooks colored in. kamloops to lean a

plural /   daybreak slowed down as one line drunk up /   eyelid

worded forest /   knees by no of a building /   thung broth.

cubit larp /   ball menhir fangled /   legs mint only of beach

outlived with anything /   sound stacked to arithmetic

another arounds by a day /   hair as buried space, behind it

lies the blank drink of a knock /   words off of a singer

(eyeline teal) /   rupp apostrophe /   each decide a down as

proletariat /   enough ocean had to be ended somewhere /   tennis

balls down to music /   lengs cleft /   skin in low dried between

"waver"

insides as please
(m'olive of it)
daughter for now
built in cloud
(orang attest) nmendous
nill off boileds
day-black (mane-balled)
piecer
standstill on toff
drogue boone
a short left to tell
its dust holed
movie inters
(mew'n) no inkle
fact storked
inside the color
melt of apart amish
dromeda pleg
old time
next to spatter
the sea from some lean
throw browner (ang plagiarist)
tipi,spad   chevron,droves
lieder blesh
blem fixity

a pudding band of highway
smarture
tine   knock
sawed medley
dennes jitter
alask can't spilts
thame ink
one's luke bacteria
sky without touch (minded)
pictory
tarsal
ahead is tied to speck
quites in ones
cleans ocree

        ellener at angle
        stackeds dowler
        sound back in
        landmine tar
        additional thomist
        'rp mose
        drim saltery
          every folded jute
            pathé wooded up
              oatl curvature
          line of grist
          stand to
          glued bunt
          pudd (via did) pale value

      bored off clung emblem
    copper in black divides
  sine par (they outlook)
    cloud olick
      take underlined about psychoanalysis
        quiets apart thing
          orch'll
            ohm nuncer
          ponded qualm
        age off film pounce
    euphem posy
  flam parted nicetie langer
      bunt dirk
        tint'l named (glance
          sud) to downs
            per adjective, too cement
        doesn't earth
      belong where the inside is
    a wall Natick unsalted
  block'll
    inlet
    law'm
        far off sterling
          ear by minus gray mysterioso
          tide solder

                        46

romed clewed
    found off staying
        through but for inches
        red odd-nouned
        inents
        each bottom to their say
    paper money skills
    (crag in tropee)
altoon
    brick gong
    caster
        put muscles
        time as after
        make in eye
            (negged)
        mulcher
    dreyfusard
    away at bends
(farm along by pea)
slowed blue off
    cent quog
        a boy's given name,
        chapters to time
            roughage on television
        a huge fill with what i heard
    more in just to line

    that hill of dried color, from three
    middling washed off
Quaderni del
    Carcere
        no melt of its last
        (glazed-of-
        the-mill)
            upon argument
        brickle
    landlord
    whole-thighed
    Bildungsroman
pile of seeds
sawed-in roentgen
chanson de geste

view of river
locked up in parboil
geoler murn
muddle dispenser
(sp'ork)
reach
browned
cloon
tine
caulk,
clear of stint
chocked. decline in idaho
what alack bride
penmanship inside out
brained on quits
talkskim
truffle b'lask

thinking about lining sound
an arm of air
easel hilled algol forth
gulf mell
(sunken
masking) idée crunk
Absalom in ball jeff
clave dist
any motion of counted landscape
heard at once
enough parched show
storatives
a famous painter written down
(sideburn repeats)
skew as a porch duration
echoed meg
heat's not alphabetical
about pages
lasted where outside is
earred

(tarner)
breaks tape by a while
kidney eries
can't relax to tallow

slanted ball
"wealth for the one that wants it"
skin placed by
no lined eggs
think at removed keys
scan lost in wheat letters
its most know stayball
can britter
of gawk
bird floor * drister ash
all the huge found in its earred
white cover
(whenever i'm serious)
no plugged snow
worked by an over
sound as a yellow through
utah in thick lines
plusses
gills
off "survoice"
bookcase full of birds

alike in a last
end s'paint
sky can't without
average to it
squig dollar
bye together in tens, line of draw
(movietone)
opinioned rounder

a later for saying on
  whitewashed milk
    eyelet sachem (off softboi
    enmastic
  a round painting, number skinned
  overheard more disappears
height done in people
  sutts. when balled
    a town as usually
      black rice
        perspip
          goalie spa
        mapple ought
      all bents
    house
   impasto
 drops of Dutchman
pronounced to target

  doing nothing as if
it belonged on an easel
understood via laker
  people see by divides
   another undergo
   with lipstick on
    no equal next
  ceil't tiner
  full of gaze glay script
personality would be merely penmanship
   brick tape
    snow forecasts arranged around
    shots charted in birdseed
    (dusked madge)
   minder dross
  paints...nogs...cleans
  thinner drog
than by hand
nosed wampum

where did civilization
  get into the argument
    clear sky
      lasts its long

        sentence redless
          landlord
            evens out Liffey
              rectangle track stars
                to any mention
              nothing lonelier than melted puppets
            cripp doubts
          (gror by name)
        sedated diem
          when i look there's
            no weather in
              row of brogue
                (headlight chips)
              a think ruffle
            address in pieces
          the dark ham
        of an outline
          (white band an evener)
            at owner's
              knocked to flattener
              (sea-cleaner)
                mev slug
              a city in England
            about oval space
          sidelong ins
        lack of mustache

    London would speckle novel pages
      "this is Shriner property"
  made of stops
      sentence broken over relax
        apple made of beam
          past my age
            called

51

              a since
            dimpled tar
          odd ever since
      theory of earache lake enlarger
          loom ocosm
            cleans in English
              simplified by happening forever
              in a bakery
            gravity pussed
            ability gesso
          mathed by
        written drinks
      black on still
    b'rose
      noddeds
        "bit ruction"
          there's no dim in that
            known to its down

                    a near orlon Naples
                    pied in footprint
                      the most doubt
                      to itself
                    red'll round its reduce
                  drape
                  farmer
                a wade turned up
              Theocracy caves
                  drui'l
                    bad handwriting
                    in a lake
                      how its imagine
                        can go through
                      the less it seems acted
                    beans will do it
                  (sore piano liquid)
                    iowan from fizzles
                    a woman in a pale bathrobe
                      holding a beer
                    a hole drawn through with cracker spread
                  where you live didn't make

                        52

the dictionary,
black hair parted down
the middle
book smelt
plug beach
what knocks after me
filling up a sugarbowl
even as i couldn't
mink whirts
expanse'll
flecks of fault
downtown to anything
makes of angry
over as a strict off
singled peen
pl
varnish
added
but listening
stell tauket
nose to Leveller
buts pitted, cule texture
sandusky beyond mural
i'm past my age in money
instead of their fell
stock still

it's her own similarity
no elsewhere at all
open until it's white
money evenly spaced
a Colorado out of
thawed talk
oceaner like answer
footage amish aparts
never mind that decide
off in clay any worth
"I meant to go to a friend's & cut off
grasshopper legs"

sidewalk lung
overhead per vulgate
plobe
melse
sudded
(white band a size)
earshot balk
fronts to a mute of it
carrot pipe more annapurna

it was only her curved say
leaving till any more
i want
to write noise
a white
out of betweens,
think off-misted
(pied holster)
wouldn't say "fault".
stills by size
glass cattle
(denominations between her work)
kints grasp
off than
cinder ink
dreadlocks pollen
seems to any on
draws as pang
waiting for a keyboard
"so much depends
on starch"
ute broils
Keats with the wrong facts
everything took place at all

Alaska averaged since birth
orange over while spoken
jelly flection
skelter elsed

sound after
brick minuses
january made from table salt
(crick has leukemia)
map clag
utter dots in a name
dreg in hundred, sunburn school
eorls, moots
thirsk
lister dilm
(when in budge)
clocked lake
editor vitae
jetty handed
nor ounce null
jority
orchestra takes up all the time
tacked cress
rye'm... drangea
stacks of thighs with sides
occurs to weather

I painted corpuscles
angles made of dead logs
lasted along my name
frogman
drops
the inventor
of some early time
black comeds
per tastic
Goodman Brown
guilty of overlong pauses
skell   boric
sidelong what's as
suddener
walled over
thawed missed notes
(dream aleck. stacked make up)
megan offilm

"not in a hole,
in a footprint"
built out of words
(headbanded)
    bent out of gray rain
    facer
      glands
        a down
          of lead
            simpled

                  choir'b
                  bunted ones
                    "knows no pain" held too long
                    eggwhite to touch
                  wolks   dring
                  (procree)
              mime slows in
            pills about Cortez
        balm, corns kleiner
            throat of a settle
          odd nauseum, mulls
            noun
              by retaints
                mawk purolator
            what's name just off quench
        career cut out from all the pauses
            lumpen
              mersol incline
                a beach stick
                  (dropped chapters)
                    subtraction along its picture
                  bents mulce
              on forgot
            omner
          black on still
          bad handwriting
        placed in

    "heart failure"
    crossed through
    James who by skin
    never put pen to paper

                  56

            piction clifford
              Coeur d'Alene
                top-heavy calm frits
                (tonation)
                  hormel celèbre
                speaking words filled with forest floor
              neog
            Baader
        within trilogy
    sideview moines
      (combed mud)
        freeze bill didact
        plastered
          apart from a book,
            career after
          Blofeld
        tock
      cancer isn't jointed
    a world of composed looks
  kettle mastic
        pointed type charcory
          across a woman
            mown out of a wave
              aloud

                bran my describe
                  flesh too kilter, caved lock
                    an iced recital muss
                  hoak of its
                    flutter from opener condition
                  malled fats
              why the weather
                wants its talk
                  before each green
                    "a library at a pyramid"
                    "plung"
                  one more upon to its start
                all the book in a fraction

saw in his eye
a cream band
of bent book
huge below
aged Orkney
he broke his off
as far as an ocean allowed

smaller down
by smaller down
coat moff
thawk peg
figurines without to
a verb
that was her own height
made out of erased space
evaporated detective
explaining wire
"blum deepener"
Philip Evergood
the average of everything
banged against cardboard years
sime include
minded to tars
behind a use
an erase about line
quelch
(hear of grow,
white out as english
soda blown doorjamb
stack'rcle
cities consist of statements
locked through
bland decker

slant tagion
what's here to tell
sentences as spoiled ink
drawn talk

enough show
& it smells like river
PET SCAN
turned around chews
something's shape,
mare as boil
where's no red in,
verbs as waves
lining neog
everything that asks
reduced toward sound
cured weather outline
TOSCA
counting the baptists
wooled nose (pages)
rounded ocean
apart from my book
a whole saying
out of her Plimsoll
bath caved in
from drink

micro entence
I was born near the thirties
books stacked up
a
wall of sucked sleep.
leams
oquant.
ceam baller, timed bonnet, sponter
menity
his voice curved in front of them
made out of bent lines
th'ine distracts
chapter which angled
(sky can't about theoried balls)
placed
skin

say there was any slash in hillside
(head lem edge)
panned wall
  along witted mung
    of Bath,   spinached
      add up,   smoothed of ball's problem

            workers don't understand
              after sounding
               (legged
                crags)
                 "julia" landed
                   as kidney daylight
                 (hardly solidity)
               tided
              glue
             geometry
            collier written to opinion
          "rexall"
        given   under
          platelet gordimer
            quil'p remove
              forehand bent mews bank
                clock odd-rounded
                 about violinists
                it comes out of a can so it doesn't think
              baseman's glove
                bad skin
                  stacked behind countries
                    over that's told
                     b / w
                       Reception Theory
                  ironed bean
                  (the gray
                between her works)
              steach who
            by skin beside

                        60